Tiny, Terrific Debbie Black

by John David
illustrated by Eulala Conner

Harcourt

Orlando   Boston   Dallas   Chicago   San Diego

Visit *The Learning Site!*

www.harcourtschool.com

No one ever thought that Debbie Black could be a basketball player. People said that she was too short. Even though she was only 5 feet 3 inches tall, Debbie was not going to let her height keep her from following her dream.

Debbie became a familiar sight
on the basketball court. At first, she
only pretended she could play. Then
she learned how to play. She was
good! When she aimed and shot, the
ball went into the basket.

When Debbie wanted to play on the high school basketball team, the coach said that she was too short. Debbie hoped that if the coach saw her play, he would change his mind.

Debbie Black tried out for the team and made it. Soon people noticed her because she played well, not because she was shorter than the other players. The crowd applauded whenever they saw her on the court. She led her team to a championship.

After high school, Debbie went to college. Once again, coaches and team captains did not think they wanted her on their teams. However, when they monitored her play, they noticed how good she was. Four years in a row, Debbie led her college team to the top.

1988
Olympic Games

In 1988, Debbie wanted to play on the U.S. Olympic team. This time, however, she did not make the team. It was the first time that her best effort was not good enough. Debbie was not going to give up, though.

However, Debbie could not find a job playing professional basketball, either. She began to wonder if her dreams of a basketball career were over.

One day, Debbie talked to a coach in Australia. He was interested in giving her a tryout. He had read that she was 6 feet 3 inches tall. When Debbie revealed her real height, he told her to forget it. But Debbie would not let him say no without seeing her play first.

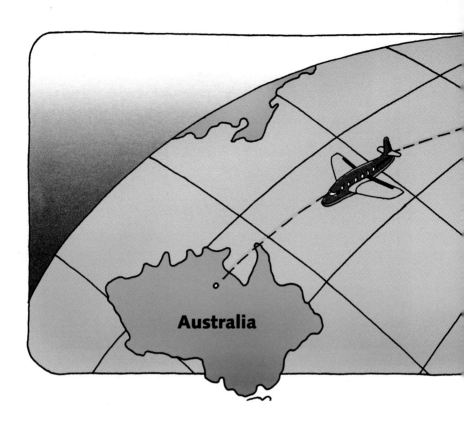

Debbie flew to Australia. Her
skills impressed the coach, and he
hired her. Debbie played on his team
for eight years. The fans loved her,
and she became a big star. They
applauded whenever they saw her.

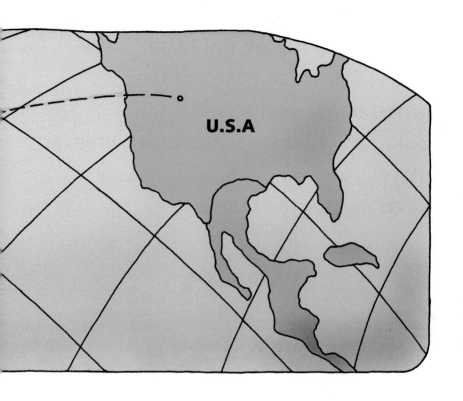

Then Debbie heard about a new professional women's basketball league. It was in the United States.

Debbie flew back home and tried out for the team. She hit shot after shot, and played as well as anyone else on the team.

"I wanted her on my team," says Sheryl Estes, the coach of the professional women's team in Colorado. "Debbie is the most intense player I've ever seen." Coach Estes hired her for the team.

Before long, she was a favorite
with the fans. Debbie was named the
best defensive player in the league.
She was also a two-time All-Star.

Watching Debbie Black play is
like watching a blur. She moves here.
She jumps there. She chases the ball.
Often she gets it away from the
opposing players.

Debbie Black's experiences have taught her many important lessons. "I never give up," she says. "That has gotten me where I am today."

Debbie Black also tells others to
follow their dreams. "Don't let people
tell you that you can't do something.
Always believe in yourself. You can do
anything if you try hard enough."